FINGER LICKIN' GOOD!
The Story of Colonel Sanders

A One Man Play
by L. Henry Dowell

BLACK BOX THEATRE PUBLISHING

ISBN   978-0615809977

Printed in the United States of America.

FINGER LICKIN' GOOD!
The Story of Colonel Sanders

AT RISE: A small table and chair sit at center stage. An old
rotary style telephone sits on the table along with
a bucket of chicken. COLONEL SANDERS
enters, looking around.

COLONEL SANDERS

Well howdy there everybody! Listen, if you all don't mind I
need to make a quick telephone call.

> HE walks to the front of the room carrying a
> pressure cooker and sits it beside telephone.
> HE picks up the receiver and dials.

COLONEL SANDERS

Shirley? This is Colonel Sanders. Do I have any
appointments today?
> (Pause.)

Nothin' huh? That's good. I was just drivin' by one of our
restaurants down here in,,.
> (To audience.)

Say…where am I anyway?
> (Audience answers.)

Oh? Well Shirley, evidently I'm down here
in_____ and I was just drivin' by and
thought I'd come in and see how they was doin'. Figured I
might teach 'em a thing or two about fryin' up chicken.
> (Pause.)

Nah…I won't be too hard on 'em. They look like a pretty
good bunch…'cept for this one fella in the front here. He
looks a might shifty.
> (Pause.)

Ok then honey…I will. Goodbye now.

> HE hangs up phone.

I just like to stop in once in a while and check up on the franchises when I can. I reckon it sometimes gives the store manager the fits to see me walk through the door holdin' a pressure cooker like this right here.

Holds up pressure cooker.

This is just like the one I used to start this whole thing. Mixing up herbs and spices in my kitchen to get just the right combination. I like talkin' to young folks like you that work for us and tellin' 'em all about how this here company got started and raisin' a little hell once in a while when things ain't goin' exactly right. I'm a one man consumer protection agency I guess you could say.

You'll have to pardon my language. Cussin' is a bad habit I picked up workin' on the railroad when I was young man. Everyone else talked like that and I reckon I started talkin' that way so I'd fit in. Made me seem tough you know. You ladies know how it is with us men. We got to seem tough when we work around one another like that. Truth is, it troubled me somethin' awful over the years so I tried to give it up, but dontcha' see it's hard for me not to call a no-good, lazy, incompetent, dishonest S.O.B. by anything else but his rightful name, if you know what I mean?

Notices one worker's untied shoe lace.

Tie your shoe there, son. We can't have you trippin' over your laces and hurtin' yourself here in the kitchen.

Lord! People have been houndin' me for years to tell my story, but my conversation was always laced with so many cuss words it would have made all you lady folk blush to hear me talk…and a good portion of you men too I'd reckon.

Don'tcha see? I was always afraid if I was to give up cussin' completely, I'd lose half my vocabulary in the process.

People always want to hear about my fried chicken business that I started franchisin' when I was 65 years old...or maybe I was 66...let me see...no, that's right. 65. Right when most people are takin' it easy. I was just about to settle down myself and live off of my Social Security check when things really started happenin' for me. I'm always tellin' people, don't you give up just cause you're gettin' on in years. You never know when your ship is gonna come in.

I know my life looks pretty glamorous to some people. And it is in a lot of ways. The parades. The TV commercials. This mug of mine plastered all over the place, and I have to admit, I've been havin' a lot of fun travelin' around the world and tellin' people all about Kentucky Fried Chicken, and how "finger lickin' good" it is. But it wasn't all gravy. I've known plenty of hard times, and I've had more than my share of setbacks. Yes sir I have.

There's lots of reasons for why I've been as successful as I have. A lot of hard work...a little luck here and there, and good old fashion persistence.

I've had a lot of different jobs. I'd work at one thing or another till I saw there wasn't no future in it, or I found somethin' that was a little more promisin.' I was a farmhand for a while. An army mule tender. Then I worked for the railroad for a piece, practiced at law, sold insurance and tires, pumped gas, and ran a motel while I was at it, and finally got famous for sellin' fried chicken. In fact, the state put me up a marker a few years back, on the site of my original restaurant down in Corbin. It said I was "Kentucky's Most Famous Citizen". That's pretty good for a fried chicken salesman don'tcha think?

I don't run the company anymore, but I've been servin' as sort of a goodwill ambassador for Kentucky Fried Chicken for the last few years. I can't keep track of how many stores we have now, but I heard someone the other day say that by 2013 there will be over twenty thousand restaurants in over 100 countries around the world. This here company you work for is really goin' places.

I learned to cook when I was just a little fella growin' up in Southern Indiana. Just a few miles across the river from Louisville. My papa had died when I was only five years old and left my mama to raise me and my brother Clarence and sister Catherine. I was the oldest you see.

Mama had it awful rough raisin' us all by herself like that you know. She sharecropped the 80 acre farm for whatever she could get out of it. Acourse we had chickens and a cow and a couple of pigs.

Thinks for a minute, lost in a memory.

My mama. She was a big woman. I suppose that's why I was always husky. She wouldn't take no monkey business from us kids either. She was awful tough on us, but I guess that was her way of gettin' us ready to go out in the world. She worked awful hard to make ends meet. For a while she sewed clothes for people. Makin' dresses for women and suits for men. But in those days a man only wore a suit two times in his life. The day he got married and the day he got buried. You married men will recognize the connection I reckon.

I remember one summer when I was seven years old she went to work in the tomato cannin' factory over in Henryville to earn a little extra cash. The hours were long, so she would stay in town overnight, two or three days at a time with her brother.

Lord, people would have a fit today if someone did that, but you see, Mama had trained us awful well. She knew she could trust us to do the chores, not to play with matches, and to get to bed on time.

That summer I had my first solo experience cookin'. With Mama away like that I got hungry for some light bread. I'd seen Mama do it so many times dontcha' know, so I set the yeast, then I made the sponge and baked off the bread. I thought it was about as pretty a loaf of bread as I ever seen, so me and Clarence and Catherine set out to show it to mama. It took us a while to get there, seeing as how Catherine was only three years old and me and Clarence had to take turns a luggin' her. But finally we did make it there…and that's where I got in big trouble you see…not for making the trip to Henryville mind you, but dontcha' see those women on the tomato peelin' line were so impressed with my bread they all had to kiss me. I almost swore right then and there that I would never bake another loaf of bread if I had to take a muggin' like that!

I had no idea then, Lord, how could I, that someday this face of mine would be on thousands of restaurants all over the world! Why…I'd say I'm as famous as Mickey Mouse!

I left home when I was 16 and right away ran afoul of one of them Army Recruiters. He was a fast talker and I was just a country boy…so…the next thing you know I found myself on a ship headin' for Cuba with a cargo of fifteen hundred mules aboard with me, and dadgummit if they didn't put me to work takin' care of those critters!

Bein' that close to that many mules was bad enough, but I had never been near no water bigger than the old swimmin' hole. Then to get on a boat with the churnin' sea below me and the smell of mule sh…manure all around me was more than I could take.

I don't remember how long it took us to get to Cuba...but I spent most of the time hangin' over the rail. By the time we landed I'd lost forty one pounds!

So far as I can see, the only good thing about my gettin' into the army in November of 1906 was that I got out four months later. Even that was too long!

After that I got me a job workin' on the railroad for the Illinois Central. First as a blacksmith's helper, and then later as a fireman. A fireman's the guy who shovels the coal into the fire and makes the train go. And I really liked that job I have to say. It was hard work to be sure, but there was somethin'...a prestige about it that I liked. Firemen were important.

I worked for the railroad, first the Illinois Central then the Rock Island Line till I was 25 or 26 I reckon, and by now I had gotten married to my first wife, Josephine, and we had two kids. Margaret, we named her after my mother, and my son Harland, I reckon you can figure who we named him after. But that life workin' on the railroad, I had gotten kinda tired of it, so I started lookin' for somethin' else to get into. Clarence Darrow, the lawyer was in the headlines a lot just then. You might remember him from that business with the monkey trial. Well, he was kind of my hero I guess you could say...so I took to studyin' the law by correspondence. I thought maybe that would be my ticket to fame and fortune you see.

Pretty ambitious for a fella with a sixth grade education I tell ya. The lessons were awful hard too. But I didn't let that stop me. I went to see lawyers in Little Rock and they helped to explain it to me so as I could understand. I started seein' how them Latin words all had some meanin' to 'em and that the law fell into a pattern.

Lawyers are kinda like actors…playin' a part. Kinda like I'd do in my chicken commercials. I have always enjoyed that part of my job. But just then I had my sights set on practicin' law, and the chance to put what I'd learned to use came sooner than I'd expected.

You see, while I was studyin' law I was still workin' on the railroad. And at that time I was workin' on a little passenger run from Brinkley to Newport and we would meet the Hot Springs Limited between Hot Springs, Arkansas and Memphis, Tennessee, and we'd have to pull over to the side track to let 'em pass. But this one mornin' she was late you see. So we waited and waited. Then we seen a flagman runnin' down the track a yellin'. The train had jumped the track and there was an awful lot of people hurt and from what he said a lot of 'em were black people.

I'd been around long enough to know just what the railroad would do. They'd send a claims adjuster there as soon as possible to get those people to sign a statement releasin' the railroad from liability. They'd offer them a dollar or whatever they could get away with, dependin' on how much blood was on 'em.

Thinkin' quick, I went and changed out of my overalls, got my suit on and grabbed my power of attorney forms and headed for the station where they were bandagin' everyone up.

Sure enough, the claims agent was goin' around gettin' them people to sign releases. So I started on the other side of the room. I told them that I'd help them get what was comin' to them if they'd just trust me. Me and the claims agent met somewhere in the middle of the room.

I got some good adjustments for those poor folk. How much I forget. But as I recall my fees alone amounted to around twenty-five hundred dollars. Mighty good money in them days.

Course that was the end of my railroadin' days, but I didn't care. I'd had a little taste of success, so I figured maybe I should be workin' as a lawyer...and I did...for a while...till an unfortunate incident down there in an Arkansas courtroom forced me to seek other employment. You see, this one fella got into it with this other fella and they started tradin' punches right there in the middle of the courtroom. Problem is, one of the fellas was me. And the other fella was my own client! That no good S.O. B. owed me money!

Notices customer at counter.

Someone go wait on that woman at the counter there would you?

After that I figured I better head back closer to home. By now I had a third child, as my daughter Mildred had been born. I heard that the Prudential Life Insurance Company over in Indiana was hirin', so I got my best suit on, marched into their office and told them they were lookin' at the best insurance salesman in the whole state of Indiana. They bought it, and gave me the worst territory a man could have been stuck with. An area so poor no one could afford insurance anyway.

But I tore into it like a possum after persimmons! Pretty soon I proved to 'em I was exactly what I'd claimed to be in their office that day. But like so many things I worked at in my younger years I got tired of it after a while. As l.uck would have it though, the Michelin Tire Company in Louisville was lookin' for a salesman.

This was in the twenties…around 1923 I reckon…and everybody was goin' car crazy. Even people who didn't need a car were gettin' one. The way I looked at it, there were four wheels on a car right? And each of those wheels needed a tire.

You see, in the insurance business you had to go out and dig up your prospect and then sell him. Then you had to see that he paid his premiums. But you see, every car out there on that road was my prospect. And with Michelin I had a guarantee of $750 a month, as long as I met my quota, but naturally I always made my quota. I busted my hump to keep them tires movin'.

A salesman has to believe in what he's sellin' and he has to enjoy it too. And I did enjoy sellin' them tires. All of Kentucky was my territory, and back then each little town would have some sort of festival you know. Court Day or Mule day or somethin' of the kind. Well, I got me an idea on how to promote my tires. I'd dress up in a "bib" suit like the man in the Michelin ads wore and I'd go to the festival and challenge the other tire dealers to a contest to see whose tire was best. I'd get two big old husky farm boys out of the crowd and have one of them pump up one of my inner tubes and the other pump up one from my competitor, just to see which tube would burst first. Course while those fellas were pumpin' and pumpin' I'd be workin' the crowd you know. Like one of them fellas at the carnival.

Becomes a Carnival Barker.

Ladies and gentlemen I implore you to keep at a safe distance from my competitors tire! I cannot be held responsible for any injuries sustained from my rival's tube should it burst and lash any of you with rubber!

As HIMSELF, excited.

The tubes was gettin' bigger and bigger and bigger and bigger and the people in the crowd would start a countin' along too, just waitin' for that one final pump that would blow the tube all to smithereens…and finally when the other guy's tube exploded they'd all break out in a howl of laughter and applause.

We'd moved down to Kentucky by this time. I always did prefer to live in a small town, so first we lived in Winchester, then we moved down to Camp Nelson in Jessamine County.

It was an awful pretty farm with a creek runnin' beside it. We'd have these big shindigs, or "big feeds" I'd call 'em. I'd invite my tire dealers down from Cincinnati and up that way, and they'd come for the weekends. They loved it too, watchin' them hillbillies have a good time down there. Those people who lived along the Kentucky River were a little bit different don'tcha see?

Anyway, near the foot of the hill was this old swingin' bridge that went across the valley to the other side. My place was down below the cliff on the opposite side of the creek. One day when I was crossin' that bridge it gave way with me…well, I lived obviously, but that was the end of my new car and without transportation, the end of my position with Michelin.

So I was out of a job, again, and havin' to hitchhike all over the place. One day a fella in a big ol' Cadillac stopped and picked me up. Turned out he was a General Manager of Standard Oil Company of Kentucky. We got to talkin' and hit it off pretty good. Turned out he had a gas station there in Jessamine County that wasn't doin' too good. Sure enough he asked me if I'd take it over.

I've always been a big believer in hard work, but sometimes bein' in the right place at the right time don't hurt none.

This was a real turnin' point in my career. That service station in Nicholasville gave me the first opportunity I had to control my own destiny you might say.

But the thing was, it was the poorest gas station in town. Seemed like everybody just passed my corner and didn't stop. Then I got me an idea. You see, I had traveled up north a lot with my job at Michelin. I'd seen a place up in Portsmouth, Ohio that would clean a person's windshield when they stopped in for gas. So that's what I took to doin'! An old farmer would pull into the gas pump and before he could get out of his car I'd be wipin' his windshield and fillin' his radiator. I suppose I done the first windshield wipin' that was ever done in Kentucky! I even took it a step further. I had me a little whisk broom that I stuck in my hip pocket and I'd sweep the dirt out of the floorboard for folks.

You better believe that extra work paid off too! Before long we were pumpin' more gas that any station in Kentucky! It just goes to show you how much people pay attention to that sort of extra service. Don't be afraid to go that extra mile. People remember that.

I had a good business there for a long, long time...until the panic of 1929, when we had the market crash...and right on it's heels came a drought in that area which made things worse. It was so bad that all of them farmers I had credited out gasoline to went broke. And they weren't the only ones.

You might think I would've got discouraged at that point, but I wasn't. I believed that any failure I had gave me an opportunity to start over again, and try something new. That's where that persistence comes in.

So there I was, flat busted. But I knew how to run a gas station, and the Shell Oil Company said they had a good location for me down in Corbin, Kentucky. It was right on a north south road, US 25.

That was a pretty busy stretch of highway in them days. Tourists, truckers and "drummers" would stop in there all the time. A "drummer" is another name for a salesman you see. They would always be complainin' that there wasn't a decent place to eat around there. That comment stuck in my mind, and it gave me an idea.

The one thing I could always do well was cook! I figured I couldn't do no worse than those other places around Corbin there. See, I had this little room off the main office…about twelve by fifteen feet I reckon. I used it for storage. So I went out and I bought a piece of linoleum and put it on the floor. I didn't have no money to buy furnishings, so I just brought out our old dining room table and chairs and put 'em there in that room. Six chairs was all we had. So, I started cookin' meals for anyone who wanted 'em.

We'd fix dinner. You know, people called the noon meal dinner then you see, and if nobody came, we'd eat it. If people came, we'd have to fix more for the family. We'd put the bowls of food right there in the middle of the table and the diners would help themselves to as much as they wanted. Truck drivers would sit side by side with businessmen and tourists headed for Florida. There was country ham served with redeye gravy or pot roast or fried chicken, mashed potatoes, fresh vegetables, and milk gravy to go with the potatoes. I always made my mashed potatoes light and fluffy you know? I hate old soggy potatoes!

Word was getting' around about how good our food was. I put up a sign that read Sanders' Shell Station and Café, but I eventually changed it to Sanders' Café and Service Station!

In fact in 1935 Governor Ruby Laffoon gave me the title of "Kentucky Colonel". I don't know how he evaluated my worth to the state, but I suppose it was because of my reputation for good food and service to the community. I'll be honest, I didn't think too much about it.

You ever hear the story about the Kentucky Colonel who was asked to take the witness stand in a trial? The attorney who was questionin' him wasn't gettin' the kind of answers from the Colonel that he wanted. Knowin' that the old man had never had a command in the Army he thought he'd try a little sarcasm on him.

"Colonel" he said, "Were you a Colonel of a regiment in the Army?"

"No sir." The Colonel replied.

"Well then, what kind of Colonel are you then?"

The old man thought for a second and said, "The title 'Colonel' before my name is like the 'honorable' before your name Mr. Attorney. It don't mean a daggone thing."

HE laughs.

I'll let you in on a little secret. I actually lost that piece of paper they gave me that said I was an Honorary Colonel. But let's see where was I? Oh yeah..we were gettin' to be a popular place to eat. So popular that Duncan Hines, another fella from Kentucky, stopped off at the Café and liked our food so much he listed us in his book, Adventure's In Good Eating. A lot of people read that book and that sure didn't hurt business none I can tell you!

Something happened around this time that would change my whole life, though I didn't give it much thought at the time.

I was just walkin' down the street one day and a fella who owned a hardware store there in Corbin called out to me. He wanted to show me this pot with what looked like a steam escape valve on top of it.

Of course it was a pressure cooker, like this one here.

Demonstrates cooker.

He told me I could make green beans in it in ten minutes. Now green beans, if you make 'em right, usually took me two or three hours, so I bought that cooker and I took it home and tried it out, and I'll be doggone if he wasn't right! Those beans was as good as if I'd cooked 'em all day! Well I got to thinkin', if it did such a good job on vegetables like that, what if you could cook meat in the thing?

Our fried chicken had come to be our most popular dish at the restaurant. But pan fryin' chicken wasn't fast enough. If I started cookin' it after the customer ordered it, they had a thirty minute wait, which was too long for most people. If I cooked it in advance I might have leftover chicken to throw away at closin' time, and I couldn't afford that. The other way was French fryin'. That meant cookin' it in the fryer where we had cooked potatoes and shrimp and onions and such. This was faster, but it just didn't taste like chicken should. I wouldn't do that.

So I got me some chicken. I mixed up the flour just so with herbs and spices and I fried it right up in that pressure cooker...

...and it was awful.

But I didn't give up. No sir! If life had taught me anything it was to keep tryin' till you get it right. And to be honest...I knew I was on to somethin'. So I just kept on experimentin' with the cooker. Tryin' to get the right balance of cookin' time, pressure and the right amount of fat. I finally figured out a method of sealin' in the chicken flavor, preservin' its moisture and givin' it a soft finish that just melts in your mouth. It's the same method you use right here in this restaurant today, though the fryers are a little bigger.

I messed around with the seasoning for a long time, tryin' to get it just right. My daughter Margaret was my official taster. Every time I'd change the formula I'd ask her to taste the chicken. Finally one day I hit on a combination of 11 herbs and spices that made it the best tastin' chicken anywhere in the world. I had the list of herbs and spices written above the door jam there in the back room of the restaurant. I showed it to Margaret and told her what to do should anything ever happen to me. And you know what? Every single one of them spices are things you have in your own cabinet at home. I just had to find the perfect combination.

To this day that secret recipe hasn't changed. It's written down on a piece of notebook paper and signed by me. It stays locked up at Kentucky Fried Chicken headquarters, and as I understand it, only two people there know what's written on that piece of paper. I have it locked up here myself.

Points to Head.

I think of that moment right there as bein' when Kentucky Fried Chicken was really born, though the company itself was still a few years off. I called it that to set it apart from the chicken that other restaurants sold. Everybody had a southern fried chicken on their menu, and I wanted people to know that mine was different. Kentucky is a wonderful name. It sure is.

I guess we could have gone on like that forever. Business was pretty good, and in 1949 I married my second wife, Claudia. I'd been divorced about a year and a half when I began to lose buttons off my coat. I could sew them back on myself you see, but then I noticed how much my socks needed darnin' and I couldn't darn socks. I realized I needed a wife to take care of me. Claudia had worked for me for many years and we got along awfully well. She was good to me, and maybe most important she put up with me.

It was about this time I received another Kentucky Colonel's commission. Well, I didn't lose it this time. I kept it, and framed it. I started thinkin' of myself as Colonel Sanders. Introduced myself that way. The people down in Corbin thought it was a little foolish, but it started to stick. I guess you could say it was sort of a gimmick. Like when I dressed up like the Michelin Man to sell tires all them years ago. I grew out my goatee and so I'd look the part and even started wearin' a white suit and string tie like the old Southern Colonels in the cartoons. From the look of you, you might be too young to remember those.

Becomes sentimental.

You know, this white suit, this little goatee…the Colonel…people remember that. They have a face to put with a product. That's my face outside that restaurant and on all those buckets of chicken. As good as that chicken is, I wonder if anyone would have ever paid attention if the Colonel's face…my face hadn't gotten their attention first.

Regains composure.

Like I said, things were going along pretty good there in Corbin, till the government announced they were building a big new road, Interstate 75, and it was going to replace US 25 as the main highway north and south in our part of the country. This new interstate would bypass Corbin.

It sounded like the end to me.

So, I sold my place at auction and got $75,000 for it. Just enough money to pay my taxes and outstandin' bills. I was sixty five years old now, and all I had was my social security check to live off of.

But I knew there was one thing I knew how to do better than anyone else, and that was fry chicken.

So I decided that's what I'd do. I'd show other restaurants how to make Colonel Sander's Kentucky Fried Chicken. I'd already been out to Salt Lake City and talked my friend Pete Harman into using my seasoning and the pressure cookers. I knew it was a good idea, but I knew it wouldn't be easy.

Me and Claudia got us a little act together. I got her a southern belle dress and we'd travel around to restaurants with our seasoning and our pressure cookers in the car and we'd give demonstrations to restaurant owners. I'd be in the kitchen showin' the cooks how to make chicken The Colonel's way and she'd be out in the dinin' room talking people into orderin' the chicken off the menu. When I was finished I dust the flower off my britches and I'd go out and join her.

Like I told you before, a salesman has to believe in what he's selling if he's going to do any good at all. I'd been a salesman all my life, and I knew I had a good product. At first a lot of people weren't interested. They didn't think chicken could be a big menu item, and didn't want to be bothered with it. We started out in Indiana and Illinois. Claudia worked with me for a while, but then she started staying home to pack the herbs and spices. It was hard goin' for a while.

I was sixty five years old. Travellin' all over the place looking for restaurants that might be interested in my herbs and spices. Those were some long days…and nights.

Put yourself in my place. Sleepin' in the backseat of your car in some parkin' lot to save money on a motel. Thinkin' about how nice it would be to just go home and crawl in your nice warm bed. Wakin' up every mornin' and wonderin' where you are with your back and legs achin' from bein' cramped up all night.   So what do you do?

You find a fillin' station somewhere and you shave in their bathroom and splash some cold water on your face and comb your hair and you go out and try again.

> HE has exhausted HIMSELF and sits.

Sales came slowly. But they came, and by1958 several dozen restaurants in the Midwest had big ol' signs outside 'em advertisin' Colonel Sanders' Kentucky Fried Chicken. By1963 we had over six hundred outlets. I made one nickel for every chicken those restaurants sold. But those nickels added up don'tcha see?

In 1965 I sold Kentucky Fried Chicken to two men. Jack Massey, a fella out of Tennessee, and young up and comer named John Y. Brown Jr. They promised to take the company to all new heights. I have to admit, there was a part of me that didn't want to sell out. But I realized that the company was growin' right over me and mashin' me flat. I just couldn't keep up with it anymore. They kept me on as the company spokesman. They got me on television and really made Colonel Sanders a household name. Not bad for someone who got started around the time most people are retirin'.

And speakin' of retirement, you know what? A few years back I got called in to testify before a U.S. House of Representatives special subcommittee about just what I thought about a mandatory retirement age.

> Stands up, angry.

I'll tell you what I think about it, I'm dead against it!

Folks shouldn't be forced to retire just because they're 65 – or any other age. Folks should be allowed to work as long as they want to and as long as they can do the job!

The role God gave Adam in the Garden of Eden was not that he should work until retirement age, but "till thou return unto the ground." We older folks can have a lot to contribute.

Now listen to me. I'm not sayin' that us older folks are smarter than you youngsters, but at least we've had an opportunity to make most of the common mistakes. We've had our quota of disappointments and burned fingers. We've lost some of the fears and insecurities that plagued our youth.

And, to the degree that we've learned from these experiences, we've gained some wisdom. I'm not against retirement for people who want it. But retirement's just not for me. I believe a man will rust out quicker'n he'll wear out. I'm an 1890 model, and I'm plannin' to work another 13 years and then become a senior citizen. Maybe.

I don't want to quit workin'. Sittin' in a rocker has never appealed to me. And golf or fishin' ain't nearly as much fun as workin'. People need to get up every mornin' with the feelin' that they have somethin' to do, perhaps not as a means of livelihood, but for their physical health and mental welfare and happiness. We've got to keep our eye on what's comin' up, not what's slippin' by.

When I work, I forget my little aches and pains. When I'm really busy, I forget I ever had an ache. There are lots of folks just like me. Workin' is their hobby. They like stayin' active, facin' real business challenges. And some people past 65 need to work, they need the money. Inflation eats up their savins at a time when they've reached an expensive part of life – when there are more doctor and hospital bills than usual. I've had so many older people tell me that they never thought of inflation before they retired. And now they have slim pickin's. We shouldn't force retirement on anybody. If you ask me, we're wastin' a lot of brainpower and energy in this country by makin' people retire. I'd like to see it stopped.

And one other thing, while I'm voicin' my opinion…lettin' people work past age 65 just might help keep the Social Security system from goin' broke!

> HE bangs HIS cane to punctuate HIS last sentence.

Listen to me goin' on. I reckon I'll get down off my soap box now and let you young people get back to work. It's about time for the dinner rush. You've probably got better things to do than listen to an old man rant and rave about where he's been and what he's done. I had best be gettin' back home to Shelbyville anyway

.

> To one worker.

Do me a favor and check that coleslaw won't you? It don't look as fresh as it ought to. You young folks keep up the good work and I'll come back and see you again when I'm down this way. Just keep cookin' that chicken the Colonel's way and you'll be all right.

> HE exits, waving as the LIGHTS: Fade to black.

> THE END

NOW BOOKING!!!

L. Henry Dowell as Colonel Harland Sanders.

Book Colonel Sanders in this entertaining and thoughtful one man play for your group or organization's next meeting!!!

This program is available for booking worldwide. Please contact Black Box Theatre Publishing at (606) 280 8351 for information.

NOW AVAILABLE!!!

Poop Happens!" in this send up of all things cowboy!

So, Who Was That Masked Guy Anyway? is the story of Ernie,
the grandson of the original Masked Cowboy, a lawman who
fought for truth, justice and the cowboy way in the old west.
Now that Grandpa is getting on in years he's looking for
someone to carry on for him. The only problem? Ernie doesn't
know anything about being a cowboy. He's never seen a real
cow, he's allergic to milk and to tell the truth he doesn't know
one end of a horse from another! So it's off to cowboy school to
learn the basics of cowboyology. He'll learn to rope and ride,
chew and spit and to develop the perfect "Yee-Haw!". And it's a
good thing, because a band of no good outlaws have captured
the good people of Gabby Gulch and the President of the United
States, Theodore Roosevelt! Now it's up to Ernie and his friends
to save the day...but beware, before it's all over, the poop is sure
to hit the fans!

NOW AVAILABLE!!!

WANTED: SANTA CLAUS is the story of what happens when a group of department store moguls led by the greedy B. G. Bucks decide to replace Santa Claus with the shiny new "KRINGLE 3000", codenamed...ROBO-SANTA! A new Father Christmas with a titanium alloy outer shell housing a nuclear powered drive train, not to mention a snow white beard and a jolly disposition! These greedy tycoons will stop at nothing to get rid of jolly old St. Nick. That includes framing him for such crimes as purse snatching, tire theft and...oh no...not.....puppy kicking??!! Say it isn't so Santa! Now it's up to Santa's elves to save the day! But Santa's in no shape to take on his stainless steel counterpart! He'll have to train for his big comeback. Enter Mickey, one of the toughest elves of all time! He'll get Santa ready for the big showdown! But it's going to mean reaching deep down inside to find "the eye of the reindeer"!

NOW AVAILABLE!!!

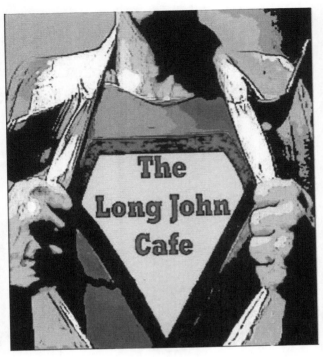

At the edge of the universe sits The Long John Cafe. A place where the average guy and the average "Super" guy can sit and have a cup of coffee and just be themselves...or, someone else if that's what they want. The cafe is populated by iconic figures of the 20th Century, including cowboys, hippies, super heroes and movie stars. They've come to celebrate the end of the old Century and the beginning of tomorrow! That is, if they make it through the night! It seems the evil Dr. McNastiman has other plans for our heroes. Like their total destruction!

NOW AVAILABLE!!!

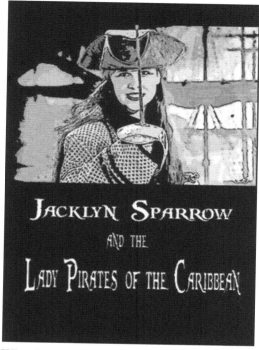

Why should the boys get to have all the fun?

Jacklyn Sparrow and the Lady Pirates of the Caribbean is our brand new swashbuckling pirate parody complete with bloodthirsty buccaneers in massive sword clanking battle scenes!! A giant wise cracking parrot named Polly!! Crazy obsessions with eye liner!! And just who is Robert, the Dreaded Phylum Porifera??

Of course the whole thing ends with a large celebration where everybody gets down with their bad selves!! It's fun for the whole family in this lampoon of everything you love about pirates!!!

NOW AVAILABLE!!!

"May the Dwarf be with you!"

A wacky take on the classic fairy tale which will have audiences rolling in the floor with laughter!

What happens when you mix an articulate mirror, a conceited queen, a prince dressed in purple, seven little people with personality issues, a basket of kumquats and a little Star Wars for good measure?

Snow White and the Seven Dwarves of the Old Republic!

NOW AVAILABLE!!!

Dear John

An ode to the potty.

"My dreams of thee flow softly.
They enter with tender rush.
The still soft sound which echoes,
When I lower the lid and flush."

They say that porcelain is the best antenna for creativity. At least that's what this cast of young people believe in Dear John: An ode to the potty! The action of this one act play takes place almost entirely behind the doors of five bathroom stalls. This short comedy is dedicated to all those term papers, funny pages and Charles Dickens' novels that have been read behind closed (stall) doors!

Bathroom humor at its finest!

NOW AVAILABLE!!!

Declassified after 40 years!

On December 21, 1970, an impromptu meeting took place between the King of Rock and Roll and the Leader of the Free World.

Elvis Meets Nixon (Operation Wiggle) is a short comedy which offers one possible (and ultimately ridiculous) explanation of what happened during that meeting.

NOW AVAILABLE!!!

Even Adam

In the beginning, there was a man.
Then there was a woman.
And then there was this piece of fruit...
...and that's when everything went horribly wrong!
Even Adam is a short comedy exploring the relationship
between men and women right from day one.

Why doesn't he ever bring her flowers like he used to?
Why doesn't she laugh at his jokes anymore?
And just who is that guy in the red suit?
And how did she convince him to eat that fruit, anyway?

NOW AVAILABLE!!!

Count Dracula is bored. He's pretty much sucked Transylvania dry, and he's looking for a new challenge. So it's off to New York, New York! The Big Apple! The town that never sleeps...that'll pose a challenge for sure.
Dracula purchases The Carfax Theatre and decides to put on a big, flashy Broadway show...

THE DRACULA SPECTACULA!

Of course the Theatre just happens to be across the street from Dr. Seward's Mental Hospital where people have been mysteriously dying since The Count moved in.
Just a coincidence?
The play features a large cast of zany characters and is equal parts horror story and Broadway show spoof!

NOW AVAILABLE!!!

THE FOUR PRESIDENTS examines the lives and characters of four of the most colorful personalities to hold the office. Much of the dialogue comes from the Presidents' own words.

THE FARMER WHO WOULD BE KING presents George Washington through his own words, and the words of his biographer Mason Locke Weems. Was the father of our country a simple farmer who answered the call of his countrymen, or something more?

THE GREAT EMANCIPATOR is the story of a simple man. Born in the wilds of Kentucky and mostly self taught, Abraham Lincoln would someday be regarded as the greatest American who ever lived.

THE BULL MOOSE who occupied the White House 100 years ago was truly a man of action. Theodore Roosevelt was a father, author, rancher, sportsman, policeman, Rough Rider, cowboy, big game hunter, Governor of New York and eventually The President of the United States!

NIXON AND THE GHOSTS is a surreal drama with dialogue ripped straight from the headlines. On the night before his resignation, Nixon ponders his rise and fall, as the shadows themselves seem to come alive and he is confronted by the spirits of Presidents past!

NOW AVAILABLE!!!

The lights rise on a beautiful sunset.
A mermaid is silhouetted against an ocean backdrop.
Hauntingly familiar music fills the air.
Then...the Lawyer shows up.
And that's when the fun really begins!
The Little Mermaid (More or Less.) is the story of a Theatre
company attempting to stage a children's version of the Hans
Christian Anderson classic. The only problem? It looks and
sounds an awful lot like a movie of the same name. That's when
the Lawyer for a certain "mouse eared company" starts talking
lawsuit for copyright infringement.
Lawsuit?
Copyright infringement?
Throw out the costumes!
What's that? There's a bunch of old clothes backstage from the
1970's? Well, don't just stand there! Go get them!
Ditch the music!
What? Somebody's mom has a greatest disco hits cd out in the
car? That'll be perfect!
Change everyone's names!
Tartar Sauce! Little M.! The Crab Formerly Known as Sebastian!
Everybody ready? Ok...Action!!!

NOW AVAILABLE!!!

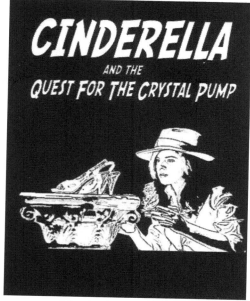

Adventure has a new name...

CINDERELLA!!!

Cinderella and the Quest for the Crystal Pump, is the story of a young girl seeking a life beyond the endless chores heaped upon her by her grouchy stepmother and two stepsisters.

Mow the grass! Beat the rugs! Churn the buttermilk!

Sometimes it's more than one girl can take!
More than anything, Cinderella wants to go to the prince's masquerade ball, but there's one problem...she has nothing to wear! Luckily, her Fairy Godperson has a few ideas.

Meanwhile, Prince Charles Edward Tiberius Charming III, or "Charlie" as he prefers to be called, has run away with his pals, Touchstone the Jester and the Magic Mirror, searching for a quiet place where he can just enjoy a good book!

Now this mismatched quartet find themselves on a quest to find the greatest treasure of all...the perfect pair of Crystal Pumps!

NOW AVAILABLE!!!

Shorespeare is loosely based on a Midsummer Night's Dream. Shakespeare, with the help of Cupid, has landed at the Jersey Shore. Cupid inspires him to write a play about two New Jersey sweethearts, Cleo and Toni. Shakespeare is put off by their accent and way of talking, but decides to send the two teenagers on a course of true love. Toni and Cleo are determined to get married right after they graduate from high school, but in order to do so they must pass this course of true love that Cupid's pixies create and manipulate. As they travel along the boardwalk at the Jersey Shore, Cleo and Toni, meet a handful of historical figures disguised as the carnies. Confucius teaches Cleo the "Zen of Snoring", Charles Ponzi teaches them the importance of "White Lies", Leonardo Da Vinci shows them the "Art of Multitasking", and finally they meet Napolean who tries to help them to "Accept Shortcomings" of each other. After going through all these lessons, the sweethearts decide that marriage should wait, and Cupid is proud of Shakespeare who has finally reached out to the modern youth.

NOW AVAILABLE!!!

Everyone has heard the phrase, "it's the squeaky wheel that gets the oil," but how many people know the Back-story? The story begins in a kingdom far, far away over the rainbow – a kingdom called Spokend. This kingdom of wheels is a happy one for the gods have blessed the tiny hamlet with plentiful sunshine, water and most important –oil. Until a terrible drought starts to dry up all the oil supplies. What is to be done?

The powerful barons of industry and politicians decide to hold a meeting to decide how to solve the situation. Since Spokend is a democracy all the citizens come to the meeting but their voices are ignored – especially the voice of one of the poorer citizens of the community suffering from a squeak that can only be cured with oil, Spare Wheel and his wife Fifth Wheel. Despite Spare Wheel's desperate pleas for oil, he is ignored and sent home without any help or consideration.

Without oil, Spare Wheel's squeak becomes so bad he loses his job and his family starts to suffer when his sick leave and unemployment benefits run out. What is he to do? Spare Wheel and Fifth Wheel develop a scheme that uses the squeak to their advantage against the town magistrate Big Wheel who finally relents and gives over the oil. Thus, for years after in the town of Spokend citizens in need of help are told "It's the squeaky wheel that gets the oil."

If you have enjoyed this play,
please leave a review on

amazon

and

Like Us On facebook

BLACK BOX THEATRE PUBLISHING

Printed in Great Britain
by Amazon.co.uk, Ltd.,
Marston Gate.